The
World's
Best Dirty
Limericks

The
World's
Best Dirty
Limericks

David M.

Drawings by Sergio Aragones

Lyle Stuart Inc.   Secaucus, N.J.

Queries regarding rights and permissions
should be addressed to: Lyle Stuart Inc.
120 Enterprise Ave., Secaucus, N.J. 07094.

Published by Lyle Stuart Inc.
Published simultaneously in Canada by
Musson Book Company,
A division of General Publishing Co. Limited
Don Mills, Ontario

Manufactured in the United States of America

ISBN 0-8184-0324-1

The
World's
Best Dirty
Limericks

There once was a lifeguard named Lee,
Who rescued a girl from the sea.
    She asked how to pay,
    And he said, "Just one way—
Go down for the third time on me."

There once was a jockey named Brad,
Who took a young girl to his pad.
    He said, "I don't tattle
    When I'm in the saddle,
But you're the best mount that I've had."

The most depraved person is Hurst,
Whose deeds are among the world's worst.
    He once screwed a nun
    At the point of a gun
To see which of the three went off first.

A cute little girl called Miss Muffet
Was sitting alone on her tuffet.
  Along came a spider,
  Who crawled up inside her
And said, "Ain't the Ritz, but I'll rough it."

A soda jerk told me his dream
Of smearing his cock with whipped cream.
  He adds two nuts hairy,
  Then tops with a cherry,
And calls it banana supreme.

A chaste female lawyer from Trinity
For men has acquired an affinity.
    She found a neat loophole:
    By using her poophole,
She still can retain her virginity.

There was a transsexual chappie,
Who thought, as a girl he'd be happy.
    While under the knife
    He said, "It's my life,
And Doc, would you please make it snappy?"

There once was a sailor named Jed,
Who took a cute mermaid to bed.
    He said, "To be blunt,
    I can't find your cunt,
So give me a blow job instead."

There once was a butcher named Clete,
Who had the best steaks on the street.
    His helper named Hogan
    Came up with the slogan:
"I bet that you can't beat my meat!"

A puzzled young boy known as Fritz
Has an orgasm each time he shits.
    He said, "This not knowing
    If I'm coming or going
Is driving me out of my wits!"

There once was a coed named Jane,
Who had a blind date while at Maine.
　　She yelled, "Out of sight!"
　　As he fucked her all night,
'Cause his dick was as long as his cane.

There once was a geek known as Blake,
Who'd bite off the head of a snake.
    He said, "My pulse quickens
    When I eat live chickens,
'Cause their heads taste better than steak!"

There was a marine private, Ted,
Who went to his captain and said,
    "Since dating your daughter
    It hurts to pass water—
I've bent all the pipes in the head."

A traveler who called himself Mort
Took girls on a cruise for some sport.
    They thought it was nice
    Going round the world twice
Before they had even left port.

A Frenchman, who lived in Alsace,
Had sex with a virgin named Grace.
    When he popped her cherry,
    She made things real hairy
By bleeding all over his face.

There once was a captain named Lew
Who sailed with his first all-girl crew.
    Debarking the skiff
    He had clap and the syph,
And both of his balls were quite blue.

There is a musician named Doc,
Who has an unusual cock.
    It looks like a trumpet,
    And when the girls hump it
It blasts them right out of their sock.

The great music agent named Tanner
Described his new group in this manner:
    "They all beat their meat
    To 'The Nutcracker Suite,'
While farting 'The Star-Spangled Banner.' "

He'd kiss and the girls called him Georgie.
They'd cry and the girls called him Porgie.
    So he put Spanish fly
    In their pudding and pie
And had the first tiny-tot orgy.

There once was a whore from Quebec
Who had a French painter on deck.
    "Your thing's so petite,"
    She said, fondling his meat,
"I'll bet you're too loose, Lautrec."

There is a young nun from St. Pharrs
Who masturbates using cigars.
    She said, "To come faster
    I use a Dutch Master,
But White Owls will show me the stars."

A boy in a bathtub named Mize
Is pulling the wings off of flies.
    He then lets them walk
    On the head of his cock
Until he just lies back and sighs.

An optics professor named Mullers
Revealed to his class over crullers,
    "By shooting my jism
    All over this prism
I come in the primary colors."

A dairyman's son they called Brock
Hooked a milking machine to his cock.
    It sucked out his bladder,
    And what's even sadder,
His eyeballs wound up in his jock.

There once was a student called Nick,
Whose gross-outs made everyone sick.
    He'd fart during class,
    Jack off at high mass,
Or stir your mixed drink with his dick.

The only girl sailor, Ms. Hughes,
Told crewmen of good and bad news.
    "The bad is the info
    That I'm not a nympho.
The good is, I'll fuck for some booze."

A great football player named Muntz
Was famous for kicking big punts.
    His teammates revealed
    That off of the field,
His face was for pricking big cunts.

A dirty old man known as Hecht
Would make obscene calls when erect.
    They caught him last summer—
    And nothing was dumber—
While trying to make one collect.

When old widow Johnson got crocked,
She'd take on just any who knocked.
    She screwed old man Fincher,
    Who has a three-incher,
And claimed that he went off half-cocked.

"*Dos pesos*," the whore told Dubose,
"Eez what eet weel cost to get close."
    The pesos she got
    For renting her twat
And he went back home with a dose.

There once was a priest from Saint Cyr,
Who loved to get screwed in the ear.
    He left with our blessing
    Right after confessing
He really could no longer hear.

A very wise lady named Byrd
Said, "Three of the worst lies I've heard:
    'Your check's in the mail,'
    'I'm not married, sweet tail,'
'I won't come in your mouth,' was the third."

There once was a worrisome daddy,
Describing his car-loving laddie,
      "He's not just psychotic,
      But autoerotic—
He creams in his jeans in my Caddy."

I know an old vamp from Savannah,
Who masturbates with a banana.
      She strokes all day long
      With a ripe yellow dong
To the music of "Hard-Hearted Hannah."

There once was a boy named Carruther,
Who climbed into bed with his mother.
    "I know it's a sin,"
    He said, shoving it in,
"But it's better than blowing my brother."

An Irishman down by the shore
Was nicknamed as Yo-Yo Galore.
    His balls were so big,
    When he dances a jig,
They bounce up and down on the floor.

The great psychoanalyst Freud
Revealed his own sex life was void.
    A girl from Montego
    Then altered his ego.
Fellatio was all she employed.

A banker from Sault Sainte Marie
Was seeing a teller named Dee.
    They'd meet in the vault,
    But he called a halt
'Cause their co-workers watched on TV.

A tennis instructor named Rawls
Was telling a couple of dolls,
    "Today we'll wear jackets
    And use Cindy's rackets,
And Susie can play with my balls."

There was a mortician named Hyde
Who had a neat deal on the side.
    He sold rubber dicks
    And vibrating pricks
To the widows of those who had died.

A traveling salesman named Lear
Was telling the boys over beer,
    "The whores in Atlanta
    Have nicknamed me Santa,
Because I just come once a year."

A tourist in China named Brink
Shacked up with a cute little Chink.
  Though her snatch in particular
  Was quite perpendicular,
She oriented him in a wink.

Old Jack chased young Jill, a friend's daughter,
Way up on the hill, where he caught her.
  She put down the pail
  And wiggled her tail.
He pumped her instead of the water.

A man who is nicknamed The Stub
Played Afro-roulette at his club.
    When unlucky Hannibal
    Drew the old cannibal,
She chewed his cock down to the nub.

A young plastic surgeon named Tony
Was hung like a great big bologna.
    The girls called him Horse.
    You guessed it, of course:
It used to belong to his pony.

There once was a girl named Celeste,
Whose boyfriend had caught her undressed.
    He gave her the shaft
    Just two inches aft.
Now that's where she likes it the best.

There once was a lady named Pepper,
Who slept with a really high stepper.
    He asked how his cock
    Compared to the flock.
She said, "You're my first—I'm a leper."

There once was an ugly old hooker
Whose pimp gave up trying to book her.
    She finally got laid
    By the desert brigade,
For a camel is what they mistook her.

There once was a cute topless dancer
Who thought she had cervical cancer.
    The doc said, "Your Pap
    Looks more like the clap,
So 'Stay on your feet' is the answer."

A nympho who dates only jocks
One night took on five of the Sox—
    With one in each ear,
    The third in her rear,
And the rest in her mouth and her box.

An old glass-eyed hooker named Dru
Said eye sockets make the best screw.
    She tells all her men,
    "Please come back again,
And I'll keep an eye out for you."

There is a strange man they call Burks
'Cause nobody knows where he works.
    In a mood of confession
    He said his profession
Was umpiring big circle jerks.

There once was a coed from Vassar,
Whose prof always tried to harass her.
    He promised an A
    In exchange for a lay.
He fucked her and then didn't pass her.

There once was a chemist named Alec,
Who plated his dick pure metallic.
    His bright shiny cock
    Was hard as a rock,
And its chemical symbol was PHAlLiC.

There once was a lady quite loose,
Whose analyst she tried to seduce.
    She said, "As a shrink,
    I think that you stink.
But couches have more than one use."

Luigi, a chef from Mobile,
Had stuffed his wife's cunt full of veal.
    He topped it with cheese,
    Then got on his knees
And ate the world's best Roman meal.

In Russia a vice cop named Talzoff
Screws most of the whores that he hauls off.
    One night he laid four,
    And his nuts hit the floor.
They actually fucked both his balls off.

There once was a monk from the abbey,
Whose past was decidedly shabby.
    He probed the interior
    Of the mother superior
And found it surprisingly scabby.

There once was a harelip named Seth,
Who lisped when he got short of breath.
　　He said, "When my penith
　　Is at its true zenith,
I can't help but whip it to death!"

A transvestite from downtown Poughkeepsie
Had partied and got rather tipsy.
　　He wandered on stage
　　And soon was the rage
As the lead in the musical *Gypsy*.

An old Roman ruler named Nero
Historians have rated a zero.
     They all say he fiddled,
     But really he diddled.
In my book that makes him a hero.

A horny old priest from St. Paul's
Had bought two inflatable dolls.
     His cock was so loaded
     The first one exploded
And blew off his prick and his balls.

A submarine man from Toledo
Is driven by booze and libido.
    He likes to go swimmin'
    With cute naked women
And get them while playing torpedo.

A beautiful coed from Wheaton
Won't fuck, but she loves to be eaten.
    She dates a young surgeon,
    Who's also a virgin,
And he loves to have his meat beaten.

There once was a coed named Betty
Who finally went down on her steady.
    She started to squirm
    When he shot off his sperm.
It came out of her ears like spaghetti.

There once was a swinger named Scoop,
Who liked to have sex in a group.
    One night there were six—
    Two cunts and four dicks—
So someone was packing his poop.

There once was a bishop named Dunn,
Seducing a tender young nun.
    When he got in the habit,
    She fucked like a rabbit.
He knew he was not the first one.

There once was a man from Topeka,
Who sprinkled his dick with paprika.
    The next girl he plowed
    Was screaming so loud
They heard her in old Tanganyika.

A daring young pilot named James
Was bored with the common love games.
    So he set a match
    To his ladyfriend's snatch
And proceeded to go down in flames.

A fraternity brother named Crouse
Was telling the guys in the house,
"I take a firm stand
That a boob in the hand
Is better than two in the blouse."

A bright young attorney named Chase
Defended a girl on a case.
    He said, "You've no money,
    But if we win, honey,
I'd like you to sit on my face."

An attached Siamese twin from St. Paul
Was banging his sister last fall.
    "Now that we've grown up,"
    He said with his bone up,
"It's not a bad life after all."

A waitress who works at the Stein
Will sing if you buy her some wine.
    Any number she'll do
    That you ask her to,
But her favorite is still sixty-nine.

There once was an ugly old whore,
Who worked in a dirty-book store.
    When boys watched the flicks,
    She fondled their dicks
And sucked them right off on the floor.

There is a great juggler named Slick,
Who does a remarkable trick.
    Ten doughnuts he throws
    In the air with his toes
And catches them all on his dick.

There once was a bum called Sylvester,
Whose peter had started to fester.
    He'd screwed an old hag
    With a used plastic bag.
It must have been old Polly Esther.

A traveling salesman named Fife
Got a chastity belt for his wife.
  The locksmith named Lee
  Made a duplicate key,
And he had the time of his life.

There was an astrologer, Scott,
Who met a cute girl on a yacht.
    He said "I'm a Taurus."
    Then felt her clitoris
And told her, "A Virgo you're not!"

There once was a man called McNichol,
Whose pecker looked just like a pickle.
    His girlfriend in Philly
    Had called it a dilly
But claimed that it made her throat tickle.

There once was a man from North Platte,
Who fell in a brewery vat.
    He drank it all dry
    Without getting high
And asked where the men's room was at.

There once was a girl from Versailles
Who played with herself on the sly.
    She started to come
    And stuck in her thumb
And said, "What a bad girl am I!"

A tight end who played Notre Dame
Fell down in the end zone with shame.
    But a fast bullet pass
    Lodged right up his ass,
And that's how he won the big game.

A lady in York, Pennsylvania,
Was treated for mild dipsomania.
    She screwed her physicians
    In eight new positions.
Prognosis is now nymphomania.

There once was a sexy young WAF,
Who answered her new chief of staff,
    "Well, sir, if I may,
    I'll meet you halfway—
Let's try thirty-four and a half."

At the movies a joker named Capp
Had a big popcorn box in his lap.
    His date was not wise
    To impending surprise,
'Cause his dick was right under the flap.

We once met a couple named Morris,
Who put on a circus show for us.
  They took off their clothes
  And hung by their toes
And fucked to the whole *Anvil Chorus.*

There once was a priest from Saint Hessian
Who lived with his only transgression.
  He thought it was neat
  To pound on his meat
While hearing wild tales at confession.

An old stand-up comic named Stokes
Was picking his nose between jokes.
 We started to go,
 And he said to us, "Whoa!
There's plenty for all of you folks!"

An astronomy teacher named Janus
Suggested, while trying to train us,
 "The study of stars
 Is not learned in bars,
I urge you to look up Uranus."

There once was a man from Beirut,
Whose peter looked just like a flute.
 The girls liked to blow it,
 And wouldn't you know it,
He always goes off on a toot.

A boy on the Wabash named Hugh
Asked his boating companion to screw.
 While she got a cocking,
 The boat started rocking—
The best way to Tippecanoe!

There once was a coed called Nola
Who crashed a big bash at Loyola.
    Although uninvited,
    Her host ws delighted.
She brought rubber sheets and Mazola.

There once was an old Lambda Chi
Who just joined the club called "Mile High."
    He said, "That was sweet,
    At ten thousand feet.
Your cockpit's the best in the sky!"

That horny old rabbit out there
Was eyeing the does at the fair.
He said, "Even money
I'll lay every bunny
Unless she's a prepubic hare."

A soldier who's stationed at Bragg
Confirmed that he's really a fag.
    One night he drank heavily
    And showed up for reveille
The following day in full drag.

A Japanese whore in Milwaukee
First serves all her clients some saki.
    But they don't get laid
    Until they have paid.
She tells them, "No tickee, no cockee."

A horny old priest from Saint Greer
Bought plastic vaginas last year.
    When asked about wrappings,
    He said, "Cool the trappings;
I think that I'll eat them right here!"

There once was a boy from the farm,
Whose dick was as long as his arm.
    The girls at his school
    Could not take his tool,
So he stayed after class with the marm.

There once was an escort named Sy,
Whose company the ladies would buy.
    But they found that his trick
    Was not a big dick,
Just a knackwurst he taped to his thigh.

There once was a swinger named Lyle,
Who told of group sex in grand style:
    "It's anything goes—
    Just take off your clothes
And everyone get in a pile!"

A call girl from Rome known as Lisa
Will take MasterCard also Visa.
    She'll even take checks
    For real kinky sex
Performed in the Tower of Pisa.

A call girl who stays at the Ritz
Has three of the loveliest tits.
    Two you can feel of
    And one make a meal of
Long after your limp pecker quits.

A counterfeit master named Phil
Was caught with a queer in Brazil.
    Behind his new press
    They found a pink dress
And the plate for a three-dollar bill.

A dentist named Dr. McGraw
Got hard working on a girl's jaw.
    He said, "Open wide,"
    Then shoved it inside,
And all she could do was say, "Ahh!"

There once was a poodle named Duffer,
Whose mistress had taught him to muff her.
    His tongue would get tender;
    He then would up-end her
And dog-fashion he would flat stuff her.

A newlywed jogger named Clyde
Got hard running back of his bride.
    He pulled up so near her
    He started to spear her.
They say that she took it in stride.

A broke Western bar owner, Mull,
Just changed his mechanical bull
    From a bucking machine
    To a fucking machine,
And now every night he is full.

A newlywed couple named Mattick
Heard trampolines are quite ecstatic,
    They yelled, "What a feeling!"
    Then crashed through the ceiling.
He polished her off in the attic.

A limerick writer named Pickett
Was hung so damn well he could lick it.
    "That guy in Nantucket,"
    He said, "better suck it,
Or right in his ear I will stick it!"

A young Down East pilot named Sanger
Was decked by a girl in the hangar.
    She asked where in Maine
    He was flying his plane,
And he said he was going to Bangor.

A well-endowed swimmer named Whipple
Just won her third race for a triple.
    The crawl was no cinch—
    She won by an inch—
But the breast stroke she won by a nipple.

There once was a butcher named Seaver,
Who went out to get some strang beaver.
    His wife caught him cheating
    And broke up their "meating,"
Then cut off his dick with a cleaver.

The madam who runs the old Crown
Just likes to put "tin badges" down.
    She said, "I don't care if
    You call him the sheriff,
I've got the best posse in town."

There once was a golfer named Satch,
Whose tee shot went wide in a match.
    It bounced in the crowd,
    And a girl screamed aloud,
"That damn thing went right up my snatch!"

A coed from Temple named Donna
Got stoned on her first marijuana.
    She fucked herself silly
    At a frat house in Philly
And swallowed a dozen piranha.

A buxom cashier named Lenore
Caught both her big tits in the drawer.
    When she worked them free,
    Her boss said with glee,
"I'll rub them; they've got to be sore."

A gadget collector named Mantz
Brought home a mchine made in France.
    Now, this is no snow job—
    It gives you a blow job
And stuffs your dick back in your pants.

There once was a man from Great Falls
Who bragged of his big prick and balls.
    He told a companion,
    "I'll fuck the Grand Canyon
If you Vaseline both the walls!"

A zoo keeper known as Old Ace
Had screwed every beast in the place.
    He bragged to his staff
    That he taught the giraffe
To sit on the elephant's face.

A traveling salesman who calls
On sporting-goods stores in the malls
    Says, "Wilson's my name,
    And golf is my game.
I'd like you to handle my balls."

There was a marine in the Corps
Who stepped on a mine during war.
    Montezuma's great halls
    Were struck by his balls
And his dick's on a Tripoli shore.

A doctor who works in Centralia
Was blessed with superb genitalia.
    Achieving erection,
    He said, "This injection
    Is good for whatever might ail ya!"

A Harvard professor named Zachary
Was sucked off whlie reading from Thackeray.
When he started to come
He dipped it in rum
And gave her a peach of a daiquiri.

There once was a nun at St. Gorgon
Pursuing a priest they called Morgan.
She chased him right through
Almost every pew
And caught him in front by the organ.

A Hollywood actor named Jake
Was missing right after a take.
    The cast gathered round him
    The moment they found him
Face down in Veronica Lake.

A bookkeeper known as Miss Gentry
Had two men in bed out at Bent Tree.
    The first one she fucked,
    While the other she sucked.
Her system is called double entry.

There was a marine in the Corps
Who stepped on a mine during war.
    Montezuma's great halls
    Were struck by his balls
And his dick's on a Tripoli shore.

A doctor who works in Centralia
Was blessed with superb genitalia.
    Achieving erection,
    He said, "This injection
    Is good for whatever might ail ya!"

I know a cute pool shark named Dot,
Who makes a spectacular shot.
    Whenever she's able,
    She'll run the whole table
By shooting the ball from her twat.

There once was a statue named *Venus*
Who told me to keep this between us.
    She said, "This sounds corny,
    But I'm so damned horny,
I'd cut off both arms for some penis."

There once was a sailor named Gunder,
Whom girls call "the man from down under."
    He's not from Australia,
    But his genitalia
Are all in his tongue, so no wonder!

The Virgin told Joseph, "Don't tarry.
We have all this Kotex to carry."
    He said, "I'll anoint
    With vodka your joint
And drink the world's first Bloody Mary."

There once was a faggot named Ray
Who butt-fucked old Ernie one day.
    His voice not the sternest,
    He said, half in Ernest,
"To think that some folks call me gay!"

A student from South Carolina
Was buying a rubber vagina.
    He said, "At first glance,
    The way this thing slants,
It must be imported from China."

A Bronx plastic surgeon named Roark
Can double the length of your dork.
    At a thousand an inch,
    The doc is a cinch
To own the whole town of New York.

A French boy, whose name is Pierre,
Engaged in a family affair.
　　He and big brother
　　Were gang banging Mother,
While Sis sucked off Dad in his chair.

A medic who served at Fort Ord
Had earned the Great Bushwhacker Sword.
　　Right after Pearl Harbor
　　They made him a barber
Up in the maternity ward.

A movie producer named Vince
Plied a starlet with ten creme de menthes.
    Right after he inked her
    He parted her sphincter,
And she takes it there ever since.

A young German boy, Simple Simon,
Was known by the girls as Herr Pie Man.
    His favorite was cherry
    'Cause he liked to bury
His tongue all the way to the hymen.

There once was a young boy called Lancelot,
Who liked to take girls out to dance a lot.
    'Twas not for the dipping
    Or real fancy tripping
But just to get into their pants a lot.

There once was a man from Eau Claire,
Whose penis was perfectly square.
    His wife's V-shaped pubic
    Was reshaped so cubic,
It looked like a box framed with hair.

A modern inventor named Gene
Improved on the fucking machine.
    It goes French or Greek
    And won't ever squeak
As long as you use Vaseline.

The wife of a thirsty old vicar
Is angry because he won't dick her.
　　He pours Bull from Schlitz
　　On her snatch and her tits,
Then says, "I'm the world's best malt licker."

There once was a youngster named Howard,
Whose sister he just had deflowered.
　　She bitched to her mother
　　About her dumb brother
And said, "I had told him *devoured*."

There once was a girl quite perplexed
Because she was called oversexed.
     She screwed a battalion,
     Two bulls and a stallion,
And all she could say was, "Who's next?"

A sheriff from old Gila Bend
Would cornhole his buddy's best friend.
     He said, "In this county
     I'm just like a Mountie—
I will get my man in the end."

A weight-lifting lady named Hatch
Told newsmen before a big match,
  "I press twice my weight,
  Clean and jerk simply great,
But wait till you guys see my snatch."

A horny old chef known as Skinner
Had screwed all the liver for dinner.
    I heard a girl state,
    "Your meal was just great.
The gravy tonight was a winner!"

There once was a man from Hong Kong,
Who had a big, luminous dong.
    "You light up my life,"
    Said his satisfied wife,
" 'Cause your pecker's at least two feet long."

There once was a frosh from Cornell
Who said his first piece was pure hell.
    Now, this is no crap—
    He got syph and the clap
And he knocked up his sister as well.

A newspaper printer named Jess
Lost part of his dick in a press.
    It showed up in "Sports,"
    Complete with the warts,
Sticking right up a cheerleader's dress.

There once was a girl named Maxine,
Who flavored her own Vaseline.
 "This sure will be great!"
 Exclaimed her hot date,
"But why are you trying sardine?"

The astronaut, Captain Martinez,
Lost part of his dick while on Venus.
 The doctors conferred,
 And the verdict I heard—
They've ordered a bionic penis.

There once was a southern debater
Opposing a girl from Decatur.
        He said, "I'm all mouth—
        Silver tongue of the South."
To prove it, he got down and ate her.

An identical twin known as Phyfe
Had slept with his twin brother's wife.
        She thought it was hubby
        Till she got quite chubby,
'Cause he has been sterile all his life.

The great circus midget called Runt
Performs an incredible stunt.
    He's shot from a cannon
    Across the wide Shannon
And lands in the Fat Lady's cunt.

There once was a man they called Jeter,
Whose nose looked just like a big peter.
    Going down on a chick
    He has to think quick—
Just whether to fuck her or eat her.

There once was a queer named Horatio
Who joined the small cast of a gay show.
    He sid, "For a start
    I'll take any part."
The donkey and he did fellatio.

A medical student named Poole
Kept a corpse in his room at the school.
    He said, "Why I have her—
    This lovely cadaver—
To slip into something that's cool."

A driver at Indy named Butts
Was crossing the line in his Stutz.
    He thought it was neat
    To stand on the seat
But the flag got him right in the nuts.

A hooker from London was found
Quite guilty of charging a pound.
    They called her a menace
    And sent her to Venice,
Where, walking the streets, she was drowned.

A Washington giant named Joe
Has reason to say, "Ho, ho, ho!"
    With balls big as melons,
    He comes like Saint Helens
And floods the whole valley below.

A mathematician called Newt
Possessed a rectangular beaut.
　　He once screwed a whore;
　　She said, "There's the door.
You came, so extract your square root!"

There once was a frat boy named Artie,
Who always would ask, "Where's the party?"
　　A girl from the South
　　Said, "It's in your mouth,
And everyone's coming, you smartie!"

The great phone-booth rapist named Frick
Had cornered another young chick.
    She thwarted the act,
    As a matter of fact,
By slamming the door on his dick.

There once was a couple named Ryder,
Who wanted to screw in a glider.
    She got on his lap,
      And by some mishap,
The stick, not his dick, was inside her.

There once were two bums from the street,
Who couldn't find victuals to eat.
    One said to the other,
      "No way we'll starve, brother.
Let's eat this girl's bicycle seat."

A student who goes to Purdue
Got shit-faced and went out to screw.
    He fucked the majority
    Of a sorority
And the old housemother, too.

There once was a coed from Penn,
Who went around grading the men.
    She told at a glance
    By eyeing their pants
If they were a one or a ten.

There once was a chef known as Haughton
Whose dick was all cheesy and rotten.
    With butter he'd spread it
    And next he would bread it,
Then serve up his penis au gratin.

A Southern Cal coed named Clare
Fucked dynamite sticks on a dare.
    They found all her asshole
    Outside of Hearst Castle
And part of her snatch in Bel Air.

A horny magician called Ed
Was leching his helper and said,
    "This hard-on, my dear,
    I shall make disappear
If you get on your back in my bed."

There once was a coed from Drake,
Who spent the whole night with a snake.
    It entered her twat
    And got her red hot,
But three feet was all she could take.

"My best," said a flasher named Leach,
"Were Nixon's inaugural speech,
   The pope's coronation,
   And Grand Central Station.
My worst had to be a nude beach."

A costumed old faggot named Dwight
Arrived at a party quite tight.
    "I see you're a ghost,"
    Sail the jovial host,
"But I bet you're a-gobblin' tonight."

A sweet Georgia coed named Nance
Was queen of the frat football dance.
    She took on the pledges
    Between the famed hedges
While the actives jacked off in their pants.

There once was a sailor named Zotch
Who played with a whore's gaping crotch.
    When she claimed his ring
    Was hurting her thing,
He said, "Not my ring, it's my watch!"

A girl who was quitting the Hyatt
Announced to her boss, Mr. Wyatt,
    "I found my ambition—
    A great new position."
He said, "Close the door and let's try it."

A crazy young student named Pitts
Went all over school popping zits.
    They put him away
    One Friday last May
After he popped a cheerleader's tits.

There once was a boy from St. Pete
Who parked with his date in the street.
    They both got a ticket
    From officer Pickett—
They went sixty-nine in the seat.

There once was a worker at Tri-D,
Whose attendance became quite untidy.
  His bad habit grew so,
  Like Robinson Crusoe,
He always would get off on Friday.

There once was a Yale man named Mose,
Who went around picking his nose.
  He'd savor each booger,
  Sometimes adding sugar
Or cheese that he dug from his toes.

A skydiving couple named Lord
Decided to screw while they soared.
    They got so excited
    While flying united,
They never did pull the rip cord.

A vampire who lives up in Rye
Wears clothes patches you wouldn't buy.
 There's "Dracula sucks"
 On the back of his tux
And "Love at first bite" on his fly.

There once was a WAC from Fort Knox
Who had a triangular box.
 She'd go out on dates
 With only those mates
Who had equilateral cocks.

I just met a girl from Peru
Who likes offbeat places to screw.
    We've done it on trains,
    In hammocks and planes,
And next week we'll try a canoe.

A drunk 'Bama coed named Gus
Wound up on the football team bus.
    Said big captain Jack,
    "Lie down on your back
And just leave the driving to us!"

A new magazine called *Incredible*
Depicts only girls who are spreadable.
    Next month it will feature
    The most gorgeous creature
Adorning a centerfold that's edible.

There once was a nun from St. Howe
Who'd broken her chastity vow.
    A priest known as Babbitt
    Got into her habit.
She's a mother superior now.

A bartender at the Club Cheetah
Had salted the head of his "peetuh."
    A waitress named Sheila
    Pour lime and tequila;
Then she gulped a stiff margarita.

There once was a colonel named Jack
Who taught wartime dogs to attack.
    A Doberman pinscher
    Bit off his ten-incher
And now he's a high ranking WAC.

There once was a plumber named Scooter,
Whose wife said his tool didn't suit her.
    She tried dildos in vain
    Till a clinic in Maine
Suggested she call Roto-Rooter.

There once was a mother called Beth,
Who named her new baby boy Seth.
    He was born with a rash
    And a walrus mustache.
They say she was tickled to death.

There once was a cowgirl named Alice,
Whose cunt was as big as a palace.
    She never was thrilled
    Till the night it was filled
By all of the Cowboys from Dallas.

An Eskimo trapper called Ned
Had balls just as big as your head.
    They'd drag in the snow
    Everywhere he would go,
So he pushed them round on a sled.

There was a young sailor named Fred,
Who once dropped his soap in the head.
 He bent to retrieve it
 And couldn't believe it.
"I am your first mate," the chief said.

There once was a man named Chuck Knox
Who went around fixing stuck locks.
 When business was slack
 He'd always go back
To work his old job and suck cocks.

There once was a girl from Salinas,
Whose boyfriend had warts on his penis.
    She said, "Though it's ugly,
    It really fits snugly.
We'll just have to keep it between us."

A nudist who lives by the lake
Was bitten on the dick by a snake.
    The doctor named Marge
        Said, "It swelled up so large
It was all that my poor mouth could take."

There once was a waiter named Rich,
Who opened a beer for a chick.
    While pouring, she said,
    "I like lots of head."
So he promptly whipped out his big dick.

There once was a girl named DeWitt,
Whose breast a thrown horseshoe had hit.
    Said one of the gawkers,
    "It lodged in her knockers—
A ringer got caught in her tit!"

A horny old soldier called Mac
Was dancing real close with a WAC.
    She said, "I won't mention
    That you're at attention,
But get that thing out of my crack!"

There once was a girl called Miss Young
Whose blow jobs have not gone unsung.
    Her best is "Hot Lick,"
    Where she flames your whole dick,
Then puts out the fire with her tongue.

There was a shy freshman called Lance
Who asked the school queen for a dance.
    He got so excited
    When she said, "Delighted!"
He started to come in his pants.

There once was a GI named Mohr,
Who slept with a Japanese whore.
    Because it was sideways
    They actually tried ways
He never considered before.

There once was a drunk named McDuff
Who went out to get some strange stuff.
    He woke up at noon
    With a fucked-out baboon,
Who kissed him and asked, "Strange enough?"

There once was a coed named Britt,
Who dated a student from Pitt.
    His dick was so long
    That she burst into song,
"I love you so much I could shit!"

There once was a mooner named Bonnett.
When asked of his best, he bragged on it,
    "I once hung a moon
    On a bright night in June,
And astronauts landed upon it."

An old southern belle known as Lou
Was daring Rhett Butler to screw.
    He said, "I'm not queer,
    But frankly, my dear,
I don't give a shit about you!"

A cowboy who hailed from Potrero
Went down on the help for *dinero*.
    His fame quickly spread
    As a giver of head.
He's known as the Gay Caballero.

A man and his girlfriend named Lynn
Shacked up at the Holiday Inn.
    She poured her martini
    All over his weenie
And said, "Let's start bruising the gin."

There once was a Polack named Wayne,
Who dated a girl from Tulane.
    When she said her passion
    Was going dog-fashion,
He went out and bought a Great Dane.

There once was a coed from Brown,
Who gave the best blow job in town.
    She'd tickle your nose
    And curl all your toes
Before she would even go down.

A senior who's at Brigham Young,
Girls voted the "man on top rung."
    'Twas not for his looks
    Or knowledge of books—
He just parts his hair with his tongue.

I once screwed a whore known as Red,
Who works in a phone booth, not bed.
    "Although you're erect,
    You must disconnect—
Three minutes are over," she said.

A cute, wealthy girl from Cape Cod
Has such a magnificent bod,
    She only puts out
    To men who have clout
Or those with a big, ten-inch rod.

A coed from North Carolina
Gets lockjaw inside her vagina.
　　It always will seize her
　　The instant you please her
And makes you cry out like a mynah.

The boy told the girl, "Spread 'em wide
And pretend that you are my new bride."
　　They played hide-the-weenie
　　Till it got so teeny
There was no more weenie to hide.

An old Injun chief from Sioux Falls
Was known for the size of his balls.
　　"Too heavy to tote 'em,"
　　He said of his scrotum.
Wherever he goes, he just crawls.

There once was a farm boy named Jock,
Whose fame was the size of his cock.
  They say when it's hard
  It stretches a yard,
And even the cattle will squawk.

There once was a flasher from Reading
Exposing himself at a wedding.
    The bride laughed aloud,
    "You're so poorly endowed,
That thing's apropos a beheading."

There once was a man from down under,
Whose farts were much louder than thunder.
　　He cut one near Perth
　　That rattled the earth
And Skylab went falling asunder.

A ballroom instructor named Vance
Was teaching a young girl to dance.
　　While starting to dip her,
　　He undid his zipper
Impaling her full on his lance.

An old Irish chef named McGrew
Enticed a young waitress to screw.
    While trying to mount her,
    He fell off the counter
Right into the Mulligan stew.

There once was a German, Herr Stein,
Whose dick was carved out of white pine.
    An electrical storm
    Caused the termites to swarm
And now he is known as Frauelin.

An astrology teacher named Blass
Had said in our very first class,
    "I think that most fairies
    Just have to be Aries—
They like to get rammed in the ass."

There once was a boy named Morantes,
Who lived with his two old-maid aunties.
    They gave him a beating
    When they caught his eating
The crotches right out of their panties.

There once was a stripper named Snap
Who played every club on the map.
    The boys in the band
    All thought she was grand
Until they came down with the clap.

A jealous old monarch, King George,
Undressed his young queen for an orge.
    "Before we proceed,"
    He stoutly decreed,
"I'd like to inspect the Royal Gorge."

There once was a weaver named Blume,
Who took teenage boys to his room.
    He liked to play checkers
    While feeling their peckers.
They called him the fruit of the loom.

There once was a vet from the Corps,
Whose dick nearly dragged on the floor.
    The length of his dong
    Was not really long:
His legs were shot off in the war.

A horny old lady from Crete
Found a bum on his back in the street.
    She straddled the pauper
    And said, "Though not proper,
I'm sure you need something to eat."

There once was a whore down at Rice,
Whose cunt was as tight as a vise.
 It was true she could pinch
 Off your outermost inch,
But you'd swear she was still worth the price.

A cute hockey player named Sherri
Was hit in a spot rather scary.
 When they dug the puck
 From where it was stuck,
She yelled, "That damn thing got my cherry!"

A cute little girl from Berlin
Can't wait for the curse to begin.
    Her pleasures are myriad
    During each period
When her vibrating tampon is in.

There once was a sailor named Art,
Who just let the world's loudest fart.
    No way to restrict 'er;
    It went off the Richter
And caused the Red Sea to re-part.

"Just what are you doing, Herr Strauss?"
The queen asked while doffing her blouse.
 "I'm shaving my face,"
 He said to her grace.
"You'll have the best seat in the house."

There once was a boy they called Rob,
Who had a real long, pointed knob.
    He skewered four lasses
    Right through all their asses
And had the world's first tush kabob.

There was a mechanic named Mears,
Who worked around sprockets and gears.
    One day last December
    A chain caught his member
And pulled his balls up to his ears.

There once was a stud named Carrouth,
Whose dick was crowned king of the South.
    While screwing his love,
    He'll give it a shove
And watch it stick out of her mouth.

There once was a Lesbian named Mike,
Who rode on a Dutch boy's new bike.
    She started to pee
    All over his knee,
So his finger he stuck in the dyke.

A basketball player from Butte
Had a cheerleader feeling his root.
    She stroked his big dick,
    Then gave it a lick,
And he dribbled before he could shoot.

There is a young doctor named Phipps,
When asked what he does, always quips,
    "I do circumcision
    With utmost precision
And make all my money on tips."

A space-shuttle pilot named Ventry
Was screwing the only girl sentry.
    She started to pout
    Because it slipped out,
But the mission was saved by reentry.

A whore who lived down by the pier
Had clap since the first of the year.
    The sailors were wise
    And avoided her thighs,
So she winked them all off for a beer

The ugliest whore is old Myrtle:
Her face always makes your blood curdle.
    But why has she stayed
    At the top of her trade?
Her pussy will snap like a turtle!

A guard in a Brink's truck named Tunney
Jacked off, and he thought it was funny.
　　The driver asked why
　　And got this reply:
　　"I wanted to come into money!"

A proper young lady from Claridge
Was asked to have sex in her carriage.
　　She said, "I won't quarrel
　　As long as it's oral.
I'm saving my cherry for marriage."

In bed an old pilot named Hopper
Was spinning a girl on his whopper.
　　And if I may quote her,
　　She said, "I'm a rotor,
And we are the first fucking chopper!"

There once was a schoolgirl named Jeanie,
Who diddled herself with a weenie.
　　She tried a salami
　　And heard from her mommy,
"Vegetarians should use a zucchini."

The only girl juror, Miss White,
Was housed with the men overnight.
   Next morning she smiled,
    "Last night was just wild—
This jury is really hung right!"

There once was a king known as Tut,
Who said when he went off his nut,
"If there is a queer amid
The walls of this pyramid,
I'll find him and then fuck his butt!"

A central vac owner named Streeter
Inserted the head of his peter.
They found both his balls
In the living room walls
And his dick in a pipe by the heater.

An old southern whore known as Honey
Does something that strikes me as funny.
She thinks the South won,
So when we have fun,
I pay her Confederate money.